About Demos

Who we are

Demos is the think tank for everyday democracy. We believe everyone should be able to make personal choices in their daily lives that contribute to the common good. Our aim is to put this democratic idea into practice by working with organisations in ways that make them more effective and legitimate.

What we work on

We focus on six areas: public services; science and technology; cities and public space; people and communities; arts and culture; and global security.

Who we work with

Our partners include policy-makers, companies, public service providers and social entrepreneurs. Demos is not linked to any party but we work with politicians across political divides. Our international network – which extends across Eastern Europe, Scandinavia, Australia, Brazil, India and China – provides a global perspective and enables us to work across borders.

How we work

Demos knows the importance of learning from experience. We test and improve our ideas in practice by working with people who can make change happen. Our collaborative approach means that our partners share in the creation and ownership of new ideas.

What we offer

We analyse social and political change, which we connect to innovation and learning in organisations. We help our partners show thought leadership and respond to emerging policy challenges.

How we communicate

As an independent voice, we can create debates that lead to real change. We use the media, public events, workshops and publications to communicate our ideas. All our books can be downloaded free from the Demos website.

www.demos.co.uk

First published in 2005
© Demos
Some rights reserved – see copyright licence for details

ISBN 1 84180 153 4
Copy edited by Julie Pickard
Typeset and produced by utimestwo, Northamptonshire
Printed in the United Kingdom

For further information and
subscription details please contact:

Demos
Magdalen House
136 Tooley Street
London SE1 2TU

telephone: 0845 458 5949
email: hello@demos.co.uk
web: www.demos.co.uk

True Blue

How Fair Conservatism can win the next election

Nicholas Boys Smith

DEM☉S

DEM⊙S

Contents

About the author

Nicholas Boys Smith is a professional strategist who has seen the Conservative Party at all levels and in most parts of the country over the last ten years – as a member, activist, cabinet and shadow cabinet adviser, speechwriter and council and parliamentary candidate. He has published two influential studies on the re-regulation of the British labour markets and written for the *Spectator* and the *Wall Street Journal*. He is currently completing a major study on the British welfare system and is secretary to the Tax Reform Commission set up by the Shadow Chancellor of the Exchequer, George Osborne. Nicholas was previously a senior manager for McKinsey & Co and now runs his own strategic consultancy focusing on financial and public sector organisations.

Acknowledgements

I would like to thank Tom Bentley for having the courage to commission *True Blue* and both him and his colleagues at Demos for their excellent guidance, feedback and support during drafting and preparation. Andrew Cooper, Greg Smith and Bob Tyrrell all kindly helped on particular factual points – and David Robbins shared his ideas. I would also like to thank (in very rough chronological order) Daniel Finkelstein, Peter Lilley, Peter Barnes, Dominic Schofield, Sheila Lawlor, George Osborne, John Moss, Greg Hands, David Willets and John Glenn for helping me see far more of politics and of the Conservative Party than I would otherwise have seen. They are not implicated in this work or its views. *True Blue* would not be the same work without the advice, friendship and generosity of Alexander Stevenson, Aster Crawshaw and Fabian Richter. And it would not exist at all without the tolerance and love of Constance de Montigny and the perennial support of my parents and family. All errors and opinions are, of course, mine.

Nicholas Boys Smith
November 2005

Executive summary

○ In the United States, Hurricane Katrina revealed the dark underbelly of American poverty. There are no hurricanes in Britain. But there is the poverty. It is painfully and savagely apparent that Britain, too, is less equal now than it has been for nearly a century. For 30 years, this growth in inequality has been dismissed as an inevitable consequence of the modern world. It is time that the Conservative Party is about resolving inequality and making Britain fairer. This is the *right* thing to do.

○ Voters know British society is unfair. Their fundamental views on the decency (or otherwise) of political parties are driven by whether they think politicians care. Labour, it is thought, do. We don't. Resolving unfairness is therefore also the *smart* thing to do.

○ The generation who were born between the mid 1960s and the mid 1970s are the problem. We might call them 'Generation Gap' as they dress conservative but do not vote Conservative. They have not. They are not. They give every sign that they will not. This is the big, and unspoken, demographic development in our voter base. The very youngest voters are *more* likely to vote Conservative than are 'Generation Gap'.

O Winning 'Generation Gap' is the next challenge in politics. As the Blair era enters its *fin de siècle*, and as Labour's freehold on power looks as if it might be finite, the party that can capture 'Generation Gap' will win. These voters are the key that unlocks at least two dozen crucial seats.

O This pamphlet – an open letter to the new leader – sets out how the Conservative Party could combine the short-term opportunity created by the leader's election with a longer-term strategy designed to win power and shape the UK's political agenda. Its core is 'Fair Conservatism'.

O Britain is not America. Conservatives talk to Britain as if it is. Most voters are opposed to further market-led reforms and support higher taxes. Our policies and their presentation consistently miss this point. The Conservatives can mould the post-Blair political scenery only by re-engaging with *all* parts of British society and by creating an explanation for how the public sector can be reformed *without* leaving the poorest behind.

O Unless we can clearly and consistently guarantee that our proposals for more public sector choice do not leave the poorest worse off and are inspired by a passion for fairness and for renewing society they will continue to be comprehensively rejected by the British public – and should be sent back by us to the policy drawing board. This may mean soft peddling on some elements of, for example, outsourcing and local accountability. So be it.

O Fair Conservatism's agenda should be to 'Make Britain Fairer'. All our 'symbolic' headline policies should be targeted at this. These might include:
  – 'Fair Tax' so that the poor pay radically less tax
  – a 'Fair Chance' so that *more* money is spent on educating the least fortunate as choice and variety is re-introduced into British education

- a 'Fair Deal' on crime so that communities that suffer worst seize back control from a timid bureaucracy
- introducing 'Fair Welfare that Works' rather than merely paring away at benefits and running job-find schemes badly in the public sector
- creating a 'Fair Britain' with radical encouragement of enterprise and social renewal in the least prosperous areas.

○ A Fair Conservative Party should be the *long-term* party – the party that consistently talks about the long-term challenges that Britain faces – even when the answers are difficult. Again, this is the *right* thing to do. It is also the *smart* thing to do to overcome the view that Conservatives, above all parties, are short term and opportunistic.

○ Fair Conservatism's answer to these long-term problems should be part of a new philosophic 'middle way' we need to sketch out over the next three years between the corporatism of Europe and the more unfettered capitalism of the US. This could be sharply differentiated from the ultimately unsuccessful Blairite third way by the confidence with which it embraces public sector reform and rejects centralised meddling.

○ Fair Conservatism must talk about 'left-wing problems' in 'left-wing terms' rather than just continuing to intone a 'right-wing' focus on the market and individual freedom. Our statement of objectives and our instinctive public responses must broaden our and the public understanding of the Conservative Party's aims and missions. We are not *just* a free market party – we are a party that, *inter alia*, uses the free market to support a society of peace and prosperity, fairness, property and civility.

○ Finally, we must not give up. With (and only with) the right culture, language and priorities we *can* win. We 'won' the English vote. There are nine million 'possible' Conservative voters and two million 'likely' ones – enough to win an election with a 1992-scale majority. As our 'army' of councillors increases and as our campaigning skills improve, there is no empirical reason why the Conservatives cannot win the next election.

1. Introduction

Regardless of its outcome, the 2005 Conservative leadership campaign already has two achievements. It has brought excitement back into Conservative politics. And it has re-established a consensus for change; for 'recasting our values' as one candidate put it.[1]

Few have doubted that this recasting must appeal to a wider slice of our fellow citizens. Few have denied that the young don't vote Conservative. Few would disagree that 'recast' Conservative values must be more about the 'we' and less about the 'me': 'personal responsibility' without 'selfish individualism'; 'lower taxes' but not 'favouring the rich'; 'rolling back the state' but not 'leaving the weak behind'.

The case for change has been made. But it is a case that has been made before. Since 1997, the Conservative Party has repeatedly attempted to adopt a centrist, modernising position, and quickly retreated towards a right-wing 'core vote'. The winner of this leadership contest will need more than a case for change in order to avoid this trap. He will need to convert its logic into a strategy that builds a bridge to the British people as his three predecessors have tried and failed to do.

Over the next three years, this will require both broadening and sharpening our new definition of Conservative values. Broadening because, by 2009, we will need a coherent range of realistic policies to appeal to the country. But sharpening because we will need to be able to encapsulate our recast values in one word. What is it that we are? What is it that we are not?

If we get this new focus correct Conservatives can define the post-Blair era. For as Tony Blair's authority, his bridge to the electorate, begins to crumble, his achievements are beginning to look, perhaps above all to him, as if they might be alarmingly thin. He promised prizes for all – a more competitive and a more equal Britain. He has achieved neither. Britain is empirically less competitive and less equal than when he first walked into Downing Street. These are both indisputable facts.[2]

Against this changing landscape, this pamphlet argues that the new Conservatism has, above all, to be fair. Fair because Britain is, unquestionably, not. Fair because the government's centralised meddling has not been. Fair because it is a value the British understand and appreciate. Fair because it is a value that is true to the deepest and longest traditions of Conservatism. Fair, in the last analysis, because we need to extend the successes of the 1980s to everyone, not just the fortunate few.

New Labour has failed to achieve its own ends. With the right focus and the right values there is no reason why the Conservatives cannot redefine politics. But to do so, we must recognise the central and common challenges of politics as British society changes, rather than revert to a set of solutions apparently rooted in a past era.

If we do this we can win. Here, in part, is how.

2. Unfair Britain: the return of two nations

One cold spring day in March 1889, Charles Booth (successful Liverpool-born Victorian leather and shipping merchant) slipped out of his West End London home at 6 Grenville Place and crossed town to 92 Eldon Street in the East End. Now prosperous, it was then one of the poorest lodgings in one of the poorest corners of the city. Charles Booth was to spend two weeks lodging with the family of Mrs Pierce, talking to them and their neighbours and observing how they lived. And he was to spend much of the next nine years researching the 'life and labour' of the poor of London.

His conclusions were stark and influential: 30 per cent of Londoners lived in absolute poverty; 30 per cent were in real and sustained physical want – 'starving' as recorded in entry after entry of *Life and Labour in London*.[3]

This perception was part of a wider awakening across late Victorian Britain. The old mantras of flag and free trade were no longer sufficient. They left a third of urban Britain living in deprivation and poverty. What was the good of exploring in 'darkest Africa' if in 'darkest England', as William Booth (founder of the Salvation Army) recorded, 'the young and the poor and the helpless go down . . . trampled underfoot by beasts of human shape that haunt these regions'.[4]

I have spent part of this autumn travelling around the Britain of 2005. It has made me angry too. I have been to streets in Lambeth, a

Figure 1 Britain is becoming a more unequal society

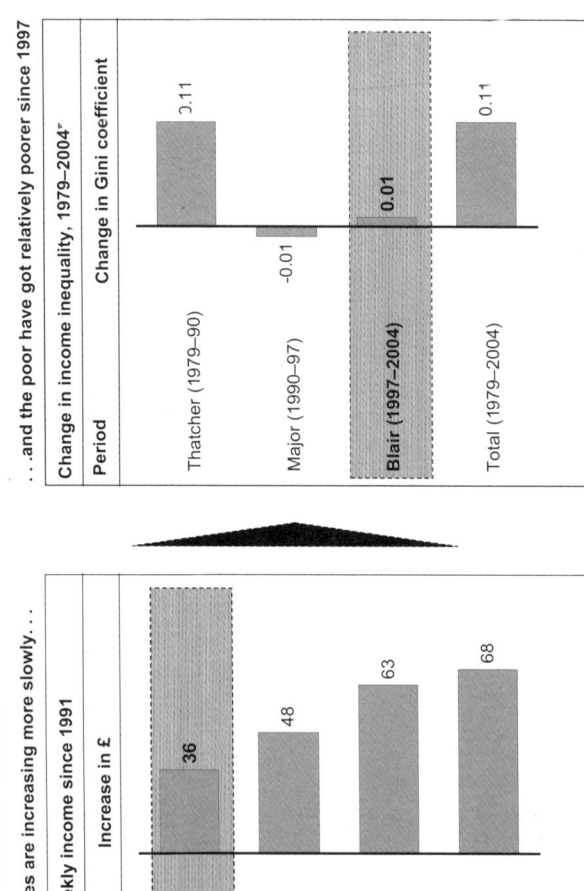

Source: Institute for Fiscal Studies, *Election Briefing: Living standards, inequality and poverty* (London: IFS, 2005); *Households Below Average Income 2003/04*, Table 7.1

stone's throw from Parliament, where unemployment and crime is two, three, four, five times the national average. I have been to Kensington in Liverpool where, in stark contrast to its namesake, shop after shop lies beaten out and boarded up; where heroin addicts go to score behind run-down Victorian terraces. And to Merthyr Tydfil in the Welsh Valleys where a third of working-age adults live off unemployment or incapacity benefit; where the town's iconic buildings have been abandoned, leaking and derelict, to the rain and the rats.[5]

One point has been painfully, savagely, consistently apparent. Although poverty may be less brutal than in the nineteenth century, Britain is more divided and less equal now than it has been for nearly a century. This is not just my personal opinion. It is a measurable fact. Under Mrs Thatcher inequality increased. Under Tony Blair, for all the billions extra spent, it has done the same. In fact, since 1980 the famous North–South divide has waxed not waned. It has increased by almost 20 per cent (see figure 1).[6]

Why is this? It is certainly not because we have been badly governed for most of the last 25 years. Quite the reverse. Almost everyone now accepts the ineluctable fact that the heady days of the union-vanquishing, privatising, free-marketeering Margaret Thatcher governments effected a British renaissance. Before that, Britain's GDP growth and employment figures languished in the relegation zone of European tables. Now they outstrip them. Before, European politicians laughed at us. Now they attempt emulation. Germany and France are slowly, painfully attempting to swallow the same medicine. They have not yet digested it.

No. There are two reasons for this growing inequality. The first is that the 1980s' Conservative ministries did not do *enough*. They liberated the market but they did not give enough Britons the tools to compete. They freed the banks, the builders and the buccaneers. But they did not liberate the people from a cloying, maliciously coddling welfare system (83 per cent of working-age recipients living off benefits get stuck in the system for over a year).[7] They did not set the people free from poor education and a glut of enterprise-stifling local councils and public services so poor as to be unacceptable in any other Western European country. They did not – with sufficient courage – take on the dangerous politically correct mantras that marriage and a 'proper education' were mere Victorian vestiges (quite the contrary: statistically, the best thing a young man can do is to finish his education, get married and stay married and take as good a job as he can – even if it is below his aspirations).[8] Perhaps above all, they did not liberate the poor from outrageously high levels of personal taxation. Staggeringly, the combination of National Insurance and indirect taxation means that the poorest actually pay proportionally *more* tax than the richest. The bottom quintile pay 42 per cent of their gross income as tax; the richest only 35 per cent. The tax take from the bottom decile can be as high as 90 per cent – forcing those in it to rely entirely on benefits and the even more inefficiently administered tax credits.[9]

And with *that* background no amount of enterprise zones or tax breaks was going to shake a workforce, especially beyond South East England, educated to be part of an industrial process into 'knowledge workers' or IT consultants. In a phrase, part of Britain was 'Thatcherised'. It is now rich and becoming richer. Part of Britain was not. It is not rich and is not getting richer.

There was – and remains – a second problem. The world is getting more competitive. As David Cameron has pointed out, China is producing two million graduates a year. India is on track to open more than 1300 engineering colleges. The world is more global than ever. So far this has not affected the middle classes (though this is changing). It *has* already affected the less skilled. Bottom decile income grew by half as much as British average income from 1991 to 2002 (see figure 1).

This profound and growing British inequality is not purely – or even primarily – an economic phenomenon. It is harder to 'get up' if your community is mired in crime (the very poorest are 75 per cent more likely to be burgled), if your teachers and family have abysmally low aspirations for you (a persistent problem for African-Caribbean boys), if you are surrounded by a neighbourhood where a third of adults are not in work and nearly as many have never worked.[10] It can be done. But it requires brilliance and perseverance. Take the case of Li Yan, who started her life as a Chinese immigrant in a poor primary school. In 2005, she took ten As at A-level.[11]

Most of the rest of Britain *knows* their fellow citizens are living like this; 55 per cent believe there is 'real poverty' in Britain. Most believe this is increasing and will keep increasing. Only a few disagree.[12] The rest of Britain cares, too. Fifty-nine per cent are proud of the welfare state. Only one in ten is not. There is, rightly, much scepticism about how the current welfare system works. All the same, 59 per cent oppose simple benefit cuts for the very good reason that they will 'damage too many peoples' lives' (see figure 2).[13]

The desire to help the less well off may not always top the polls of how people say they are going to vote but it often *does* top the polls of how people actually *do* vote. *In 130 Labour/Tory marginals after the 2005 election, more voters (15 per cent) listed 'pensions/social security/ the minimum wage/poverty in Britain' as the most important factor in deciding how they had voted than any other issue.*[14] This is a staggeringly important fact. Conservatism has to respond to it if it wants to reclaim the centre ground of British politics.

Concern for poverty goes deeper still, however: 62 per cent of Britons think it is more important for the government to ensure that nobody is in need than it is to allow individuals to be free to pursue their own goals.[15] They do not just desire this out of humanity. They desire it out of self-interest, too. It is from the 'sink' neighbourhoods of Leeds and London – with the additional combustible of radical Islam – that most of the summer's bombers crawled forth to commit murder and mayhem.

The problem for the Conservatives, of course, is that they have diametrically opposed views to the majority of the population on the role of the government and the existence of poverty. Most people think (unfairly) that the Thatcher governments created more absolute poverty and revelled in it. We don't respond. We just can't talk about poverty in terms that would allow us to. We don't intone with energy about the inequality or unfairness of it all. It doesn't reduce us to rage

Figure 2 Most British people know and care about inequality

British attitudes to poverty, %

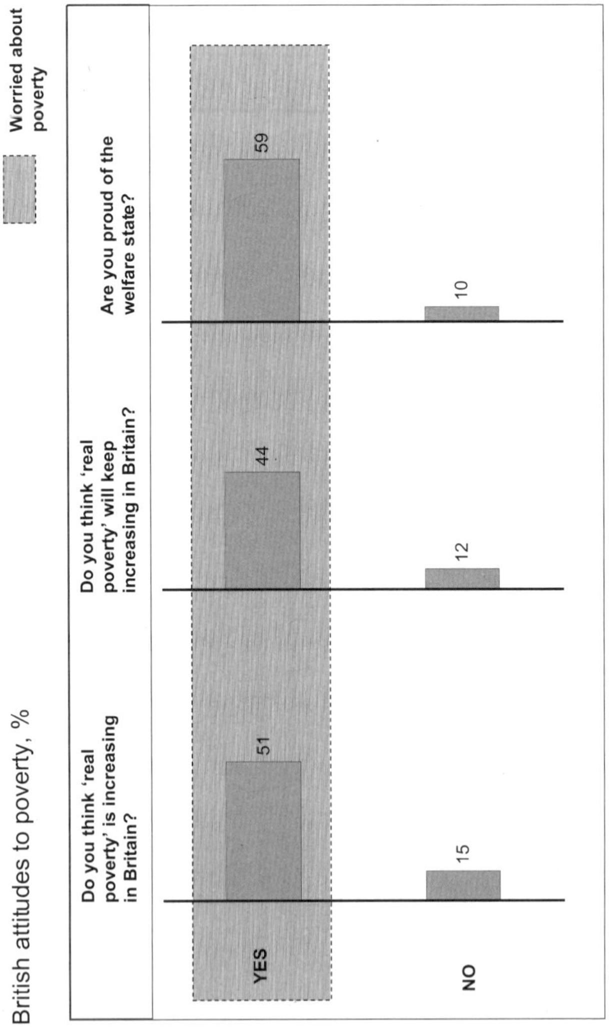

Source: *British Social Attitudes* (see: www.britsocat.com)

that 10 per cent of fellow countrymen are living on less than £150 a week.[16] Hardly surprisingly that poorer regions, therefore, just don't even think about voting for us (see figure 3).

This isn't because recent Tory front benchers have not worried about unfairness. They have. Iain Duncan Smith made it his mantra. David Willetts probably knows more about below-average income families than any government minister. The problem is that too many other Conservatives have denied the existed of 'real poverty' in the UK; too many have not cared; and too many have consistently talked with cool efficiency about the solution without passing through a necessary interval of heat and passion about the problem. From being (in the public perception) the desiccated economists of the 1980s we have passed on to being the desiccated social technocrats of the new century. Worse, we are desiccated social technocrats whose motivation is questionable.

Take one speech – Iain Duncan Smith's address to the Conservative Party Conference in 2003 when he touched on pensions and pensioners:

> *Gordon Brown has forced an extra million pensioners onto the means test. Two out of every three pensioners are now on social security. For many people the means test has made it unprofitable to save for retirement. More means-testing, more tax, less savings. What a mess.*

> *So we will raise the basic state pension, in line with earnings to ensure that future generations of pensioners never have to go begging for social security.*

> *The abolition of the means test is supported by the savings industry, it's supported by millions of pensioners and it's supported by me. Most important of all, it's the right thing to do.[17]*

This speech is full of what linguistic experts term 'concept-based' vocabulary ('raise', 'unprofitable', 'abolition', 'supported').[18] It argues.

Figure 3 Our perceived lack of concern locks us out of half the country

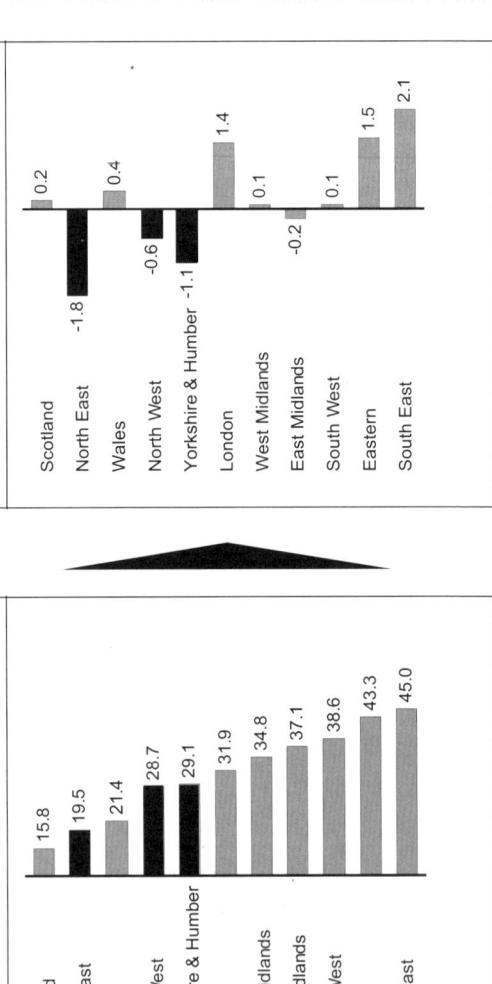

Relatively poorer regions don't vote for us. . . . . . and are not changing their mind

Conservative share of vote in 2005 General Election

Region	Share of vote, %
Scotland	15.8
North East	19.5
Wales	21.4
North West	28.7
Yorkshire & Humber	29.1
London	31.9
West Midlands	34.8
East Midlands	37.1
South West	38.6
Eastern	43.3
South East	45.0

Change in Conservative vote, 2005 General Election

Region	Increase in vote, %
Scotland	0.2
North East	-1.8
Wales	0.4
North West	-0.6
Yorkshire & Humber	-1.1
London	1.4
West Midlands	0.1
East Midlands	-0.2
South West	0.1
Eastern	1.5
South East	2.1

Poorer region & falling vote

Source: BBC Election website

It reasons. It does not impassion or emote.

By contrast take Tony Blair in 1994. He suffers now from a surfeit of words and a shortage of success. But read his words back in the dawn of his leadership:

> *It is a mission to lift the spirit of the nation, drawing its people together, to rebuild the bonds of common purpose that are at the heart of any country fit to be called one nation: a country where we say: We are part of a community of people – we do owe a duty to more than ourselves; a country where we help those who cannot help themselves; a country where if it's not good enough for my children it's not good enough for theirs.*[19]

Tony Blair had the same mission in 1994 as Iain Duncan Smith in 2003. But what a difference in language. It is what linguists call 'image-based' ('mission', 'lift the spirit', 'rebuild the bonds'). He shares the pain – the anger. He does not just rationalise that poverty must be reduced for utilitarian impact. In short, there seems little point in talking about the use of the voluntary sector or parental choice to solve the problem when our language and consistency of purpose has not demonstrated that we give a damn.

But we need to give a damn if we are going to connect with the majority of the British. And this is far, far more than just a matter of language: 58 per cent of voters think we do not care about ordinary people; 67 per cent think we are out of touch. Labour has a 20 per cent lead as the party most likely to 'take care of everyone'.[20]

This is hardly surprising. New Labour constructed itself as the party which addressed aspirations and concerns of universal relevance: quality of life; jobs; ending poverty; improving life for all. This is why 53 per cent of voters still think that Labour 'cares about the problems that ordinary people have to deal with'.[21] Whatever errors they make, half of all voters still give Labour the motivational benefit of the doubt. Improving life for all is, still, necessarily implied by whatever the government tries to do. We need to engage, and be seen to engage, with the problems of everyone, above all the poorest, if we are to wrestle the centre right (let alone the centre ground) of British politics back from Labour. This will need passion and obsession – not a technocratic discussion of choice and freedom. We need to mean it and we need to show it. We can't talk about *means* if we have not proved that we care about *ends*. Our end, our aim, must be fairness.

One final point. A true Liverpool merchant, Charles Booth had been born and lived a Liberal. His discoveries about the London poor actually changed his politics. They made him a Conservative. He abandoned the coldly calculating views of the Liberals and turned to a party which, he believed, had a wider and a richer sense of social justice and a truer desire to ensure decency and opportunity for all. I wonder how many of our MPs, if they were honest, would find a similar decision surprising today. Our mission, 100 years later, is to stop it being so.

3. 'Generation Gap'

In June 1995 I told some of my university contemporaries that I was planning to vote Conservative in the next general election. The reaction, among a range of 20–22-year-olds who went on to win good degrees at Cambridge, would have amazed a previous generation. It ranged from shock ('how could you?') through disgust ('after they've ruined the country too') to stunned amusement ('well you always were a bit odd'). Ten years later, most of them think the same thing.

This is *the* problem with our support base. This is the issue that the legions of commentators and post-elections experts have passed by and walked over. Interred in all the mounds of polls, percentages and projections it lies blinking at everyone, unsought and unseen.

Most of the generation who were born between the mid 1960s and the mid 1970s do not vote Conservative. They have not. They did not in 2005. And they give every sign that they will not.[22] This is a phenomenon that matters. This is the generation that grew up with car phones and Madonna, with 'Loads of Money' and the miner's strike. These are the children whose early political memories are of *Spitting Image* and Norman Tebbit and who came of age under the Poll Tax or during the early-epoch, whiter-than-white phase of Tony Blair. This generation, in short, were brought up to think that chinos and Levi 501s were what you were meant to wear and that voting for Mrs Thatcher was certainly not what you were meant to do. I have

Figure 4 The 1965–75-born 'Generation Gap' are consistently the least likely to vote Conservative

Conservatives voters by age
1997–2005, %

Legend:
- ■ 'Generation Gap'
- ⬚ Lowest Conservative votes

- ❖ Since 1997 voters born from 1965 to 1975 have been the least likely to vote Conservative
- ❖ As 'Generation Gap' get older they are continuing not to vote Conservative
- ❖ Very youngest voters are now more likely to vote Conservative than are 'Generation Gap'

Data by age group and year (1997, 2001, 2005):

Age	1997	2001	2005
18–24	27	27	28
25–34	28	24	25
35–44	28	28	27
45–54	31	32	31
55–64	36	39	39
65+	36	40	41

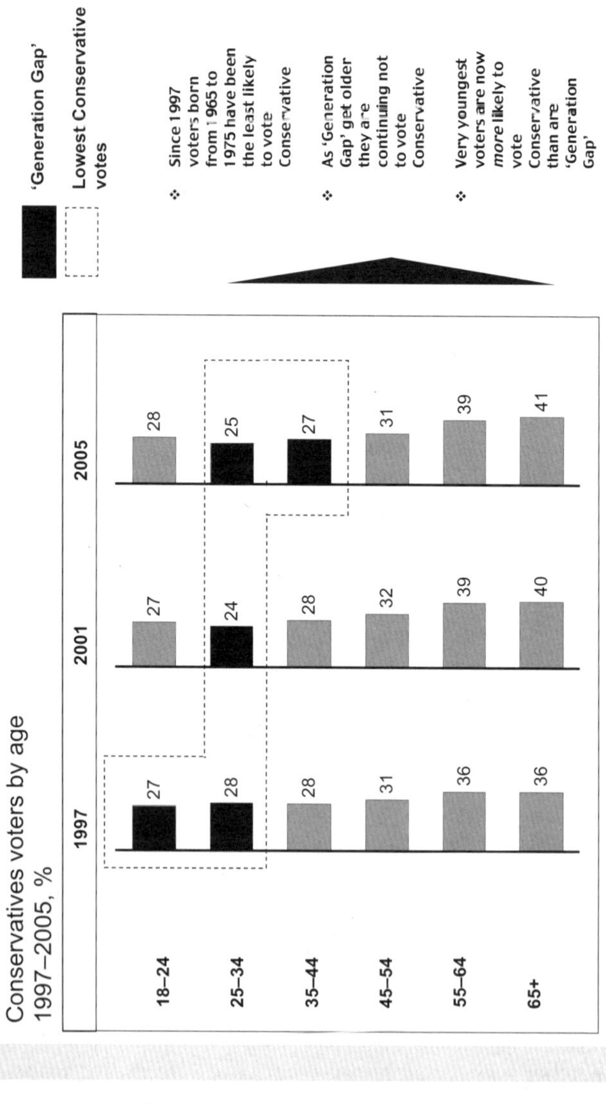

Source: MORI

termed them 'Generation Gap' – those who know how to wear smart casual, dress conservative, but just do not vote Conservative.

In the last three elections, even though 'Generation Gap' are now (tragically – I am one of them) reaching middle age, they have been consistently the least likely to vote Conservative. This did not happen in the 1960–70 period or the 1970–80 period. In both previous generations young voters started voting Conservative as the weight of mortgages, education and tax began to press. In short, as reality bit, previous generations became Conservative. This one has not. In both 2001 and 2005 the very youngest voters (the 18–24 cohort) were 3 per cent *more* likely to vote Conservative than those aged 24–35. Staggeringly, in 2005 the youngest voters were more likely to vote Conservative even than those in their late 30s or early 40s.[23] We are facing a lost generation of Conservative voters (see figure 4).

It is an important generation, too. Everyone knows about the baby boomers – the rush of post-war births from 1946 to 1948. Well the baby boomers grew up and had children. And they had them between the mid 1960s and the mid 1970s. From 1965 to 1970 the birth rate was almost 20 per cent higher than ten years later (see figure 5). Today there are two million more British people in their 30s than in their 20s.[24] Who cares about the very youngest voters? In an age of low turnouts, 'Generation Gap' are big battalions.

It is not just a question of numbers. 'Generation Gap' is beginning to play a pivotal role in national life. Their power, visibility and influence is increasing. As their new companies grow or as they take over old institutions they invest them – and public life – with a new, less formal culture and a new set of priorities.

A moment's thought and the names of significant public figures in or just out of their 30s come tumbling out: Charles Dunstone, multi-millionaire founder of Carphone Warehouse who works in Acton and takes the tube to work; Rebekah Wade who, at 37, has edited both the *Sun* and the *News of the World*, leading high-profile campaigns against wife-beaters and paedophiles; Andy Hornby, Chief Operating Officer of HBOS at 38, who has helped bring a new American style of retailing to high streets up and down Britain. The list could go on: the

Figure 5 The 'Generation Gap' is important and numerous

UK Population, by age and sex, 2003 ('000)

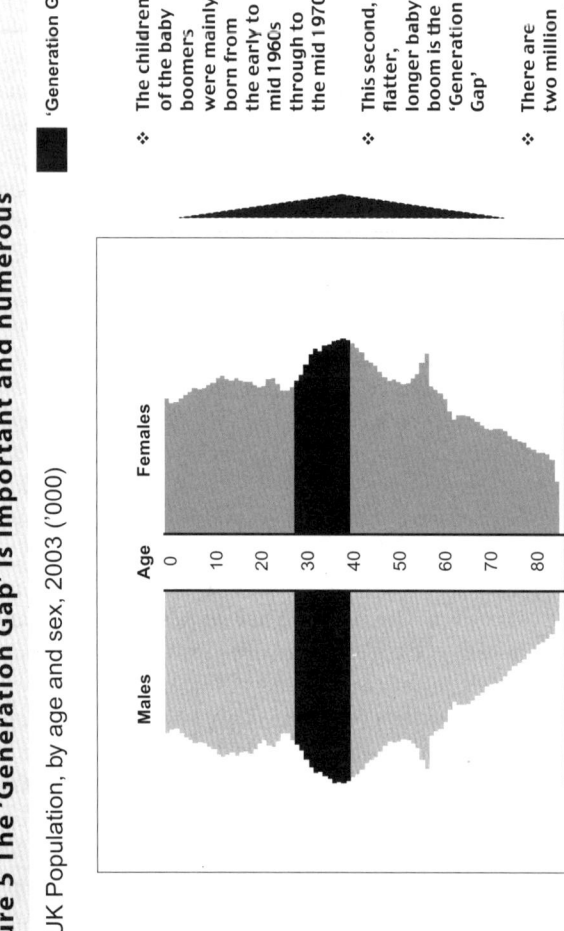

◼ 'Generation Gap'

❖ The children
of the baby
boomers
were mainly
born from
the early to
mid 1960s
through to
the mid 1970s

❖ This second,
flatter,
longer baby
boom is the
'Generation
Gap'

❖ There are
two million
more people
in their 30s
than in their
20s

Source: Office for National Statistics

directors of at least five influential think tanks; the Secretary of State for Education; half a dozen best-selling authors; a clutch of the most respected print or broadcast journalists. To say nothing of the scores of 30-something bankers and investors running half the deals in the city. Britain is changing. And 'Generation Gap' is in the engine room.

And this is why they matter. In 2005, 25 per cent of 'Generation Gap' voted Conservative – 8 per cent less than the national average. If only half that 8 per cent had voted Conservative this year, Tony Blair would have lost 12 more seats and been left with a majority of 42. If 'Generation Gap' had voted in line with the national average, Mr Blair's majority would have been reduced to 20–24 – just like John Major after his wafer-wide victory of 1992.[25]

Winning 'Generation Gap' is crucial. Their support is a necessary precondition of power. But who are they? A glance at the evidence is both surprising and familiar. Not all the clichés about 'the young' are true to them. 'Generation Gap' may be less communal than their parents (perhaps not surprising) but they are also more free-market, only very slightly more liberal and not much more cynical, if at all, about politics and politicians.

First, and perversely given how they vote, 'Generation Gap' are Thatcherite. They work hard and are optimistic. They are sceptical of the unemployed's inability to find a job (76 per cent believe they could if they wished – more than any other age group). They believe in enterprise and low tax (a majority of those aged 35 and over believe the government should tax and spend more – a minority of those under 35). They don't even support environmental legislation any more than their parents or grandparents.[26] Perhaps, this is hardly surprising. In some ways, 'Generation Gap' (more entrepreneurial, richer, better travelled than their parents, learning to work in the long boom of the 1990s) are the generation that has gained the most out of the Thatcher economic transformation.

Second, 'Generation Gap' are less communal and local than their parents. They are less likely to look out for their neighbours and shyer about asking for favours from them (only 29 per cent would feel comfortable borrowing a fiver; 38 per cent of their parents do). They spend less time helping charities. They spend less time with their friends. They know fewer of their neighbours. They are less defined by place – more by career or 'lifestyle'.[27]

Third, although 'Generation Gap' are more socially liberal and less tolerant of authority than their parents, they are not dramatically more liberal: 77 per cent of 'Generation Gap' think the young need more discipline – only marginally less than their parents. And *more* people in their 20s and 30s actually blame immigrants for crime than do those in their 50s. A majority of 'Generation Gap' even support censorship 'to uphold moral standards'.[28] George Orwell once wrote of the 'emotional unity' of England, of how the instincts that unite us are greater than those that separate us.[29] He is still right. Britain is becoming more liberal but it is doing so more gradually than the sushi-eating classes think.

Perhaps even more surprisingly, 'Generation Gap' is not much more – if at all – cynical about politics and politicians. Actually slightly fewer (54 vs 56 per cent) distrust everything MPs say. And only 10 per cent fewer of 'Generation Gap' have any interest in politics. It is true that 'Generation Gap' vote less. It is true that only 55 per cent believe it is their duty to vote (over 70 per cent of their parents do).[30] They also vote less for financial self-interest. After all, few of them have ever experienced a real recession. But overall, the evidence is clear. This cohort is less *interested* in politics. But they are not much more cynical, and are therefore open to persuasion. The British believe (like Aristophanes) that 'under every stone there lurks a politician'. 'Generation Gap' might like to tread on the stone, but so would their parents.

However, we cannot get away from the fact that 'Generation Gap' has been *conditioned* not to vote Conservative. They feel the most cut off from the current party. Fewer 25–44-year-olds think that the Conservative Party shares their values than any other generation – *including those under 25*. Even of those who voted Conservative far fewer think the party has 'really changed' since 1997. We still, desperately, need to show that we are not the narrow party

'Generation Gap' takes us to be, and that they can identify with us – which they do less than any other age group. Only 31 per cent of those aged 25–34 think the Conservative Party shares their values – 5 per cent less than those aged under 25 and 10 per cent less than those aged over 55.[31]

This, then, is the next challenge in politics. As the Blair era enters its *fin de siècle*, and as Labour's freehold on power looks as if it might, possibly, be finite, the party that can capture 'Generation Gap' will win. They are the key that unlocks at least two dozen crucial seats.

The government needs to grip on to 'Generation Gap' to grip on to power. But there is no reason why Conservatives cannot win the hearts, minds and votes of 'Generation Gap'; indeed, there is every reason why we can. 'Generation Gap' as a whole is more Thatcherite and entrepreneurial. They are more confident and better travelled. They are more socially liberal but still keen on moral standards. The key reason they don't vote for us is they don't think we care and they don't like our values.

Fair Conservatism speaks to the concerns of 'Generation Gap': not by abandoning our support for the free market (which 'Generation Gap' share), not by retreating from the need for radical public sector or welfare state reform (which is also accepted) but by clearly, consistently and passionately making the case for a fairer Britain.

For one thing is certain. Unless we convince 'Generation Gap' that we are like them, hard-working, fair people, interested in others and not out to get the weak, we can all go home.

4. Policies are the problem too

The problem is they *do* understand

Let me tell you something which is not publicly known. In 2005, the Conservative Party did not want to focus on 'cleaner hospitals' and 'school discipline'. The Conservative Party wanted to focus on parental choice in schools and patient power in hospitals. 'Set the people free' not 'get out the Dettol'. This was the heart of the manifesto. Surely it should be the heart of the campaign?

There was a problem. When the policies were road-tested in private polls and focus groups, the public did not like them. One senior pollster supposedly told the shadow cabinet that 'your policies are a lemon', and held up a slide with a large yellow lemon on it just in case they failed to get the point.

From lemons it was a short jump to cleaner hospitals and school discipline. Quite good soundbites and real problems but not the stuff of which elections are won. The majority of the public never even knew about the range of interesting and radical policies underlying them (and I should know; I wrote some of them).

In a way, this is the critical problem. In the eight years since 1997, the British centre-right has actually been quite intellectually active. There are interesting new think tanks (Reform, Policy Exchange, Civitas). And most of the older think tanks continue to be both challenging and robust. Liberated from government, freed from having to defend the half-delivered and with the cancer of Europe largely cauterised these think tanks have set to work putting together an agenda for a future Conservative government. Most of that agenda has centred around unleashing the power of non-public sector delivery and empowering public sector consumers to make their own decisions. It is based on good political and managerial precedents – mainly in the US – and is consistent with the Conservative Party's correct focus on improving public service delivery.

Most thinking Conservatives, proud of their achievements in government and confident of our corpus of policy proposals, have therefore concluded that Conservatives continue to have the best policy tunes. The problem, they reason, is the image of the party and our presentation. People just don't know about our policies. They haven't heard. They don't know that we are now putting all our focus on improving the public sector for them.

But this is only half true. Most voters *do* understand the policy proposals in broad outline. They *do* understand that we offer to increase private sector provision of public services. They *do* understand they will pay more tax under Labour or the Liberal Democrats. Voters understand our policies all right. They just don't like them. Charles Kennedy said, 'people don't want choice. They want good hospitals.' Sadly, for once, he is correct. The same is even true of tax cuts: 62 per cent claim to support higher taxes; only 10 per cent think taxes should be as low as possible. Many even list tax rises as the policy proposal they think would be best for the UK.[32]

Conservatives talk to the country as if the British are the Americans we would like them to be. Things are certainly very different in the US. There voters actively *want* to make choices and take control of their lives: 65 per cent of Americans think that they can control their own fate and determine their success; in the UK it is 48 per cent. Fifty-eight per cent of Americans want to be left alone to pursue their goals free from government; in Britain it is 33 per cent.[33]

Conservatives hope that by championing the improvements freedom can bring we can turn the West Midlands into West Virginia and the South West into South Carolina. We can't. The British patiently and resolutely fail to become Americans. The difference in views are long-lasting, profound and endemic. You might say that we are from Mars and the voters are from Venus. Light years are between us.

What makes the problem doubly difficult is that we are correct. Lower taxes, more self-determination and fewer state monopolies could be better for everyone. We are stuck between the rock of unpopularity and the hard place of bad policy.

One solution is to try to get smarter at selling the policy and to focus on the greater degree of control, local democracy and accountability that is a necessary part of the solution. This is the proposal put forward in *Direct Democracy*[34] launched by the *Daily Telegraph* this summer. This may work. More local control is certainly a part of the solution. And it is clearly a necessary response to the growing alienation from political institutions which has been discerned by both left- and right-wing commentators. Politics is increasingly seen as a separate and alien world. This can't be healthy. The focus on 'direct democracy' also chimes with the greater degree of control voters are taking over the rest of their lives. But there must be at least a risk, certainly in the short term, that the abstraction of 'freedom' will not be sufficient pull in a country where local government election turnout rates hover around 35 per cent despite a very significant potential electoral impact on local council tax.[35]

Another solution may go more to the heart of the voters' mistrust. In April 2004, the former Director of the Social Market Foundation (now speech writer to the Prime Minister), Phil Collins, addressed the largely right-wing think tank Reform on the subject of school choice. What he said was quite revealing:

> *If the benefits of choice are limited to one section of the population this has a serious implication for social justice. Here we have arrived, possibly, at one of those ideas which sharply delineates left from right. Perhaps it is open to some on the right to affect a Hayekian disdain for the alleged miracle of social justice. But it is a bit of a totem on the left. If choice can even be presented as inimical to social justice it is finished.*[36]

The British people may come to love choice. They *do* love it away from education and the NHS. But they still hold dear to the principles of free use and equality in many public services. Even though they discern the need for reform, only 20 per cent oppose the principle of the NHS.[37]

This is the route to escaping our policy dilemma. Our development, and not just our presentation, of economic policy and public service reforms must focus like a Davy lamp on the issue of 'social justice'. Our changes must not leave the poor and the ill educated stranded, knee-deep, in a sewer of sink provision. And nothing must get in the way of a clear cast-iron explanation of this. Let's be quite explicit. *Unless we can guarantee that our proposals for more choice, lower tax and outsourcing do not leave the poorest worst off it's back to the policy drawing board for them.* This will mean keeping some state provision. This will mean soft peddling on some elements of outsourcing and local accountability. That may even mean some central quasi-*dirigiste* warping of markets for public goods. So be it. The end point is the same. This is Fair Conservatism.

Fair Conservatism

Fair Conservatism means going beyond reforms in the public sector, beyond encouraging non-state provision, beyond local democracy, beyond even replacing lounge suits with smart casual. Fair democracy is a new focus on *ends* not *means*. It is expressing an aim to make Britain fairer and to share opportunity and wealth for all. The fairness is in the aim. The conservatism is in the policies.

What are potential 'symbolic' policies which pass this test? What are policies which could make Britain richer and better but which could also make Britain *fairer*? And, just as hard, what are policies which can represent this new focus to new voters without alienating old ones?

First of all, the unshakeable framework must be one of improving the public services to the benefit of all. It is astonishing that no Conservative leader since 1997 has retained a consistent focus on public sector reform. Hague, Duncan Smith and Howard all started.

None finished. This is despite clear and consistent evidence that these are the public's priorities. A commitment to public sector improvement carried out to benefit the least well off has therefore to be the repetitive core of our policy.

However, within this framework, and in the spirit of making suggestions rather than laying down manifestos, let me set out five ideas which can represent the twin strands of increasing freedom and increasing fairness.

1   **Fair Tax.** Fair Conservatism's tax policies must have two aims. First, to simplify and flatten the tax system. (This should focus on helping the poorest first. It is outrageous that the marginal rate of National Insurance is 11 per cent for those earning less than £630 a week and 1 per cent for those earning more. These are the anomalies that should be attacked first.) Second, and just as crucially, Fair Conservatism should aim to liberate the least well off from tax altogether. It is shocking that the poorest pay proportionally *more* tax (42 per cent of gross earnings for the bottom quintile) than the richest (who pay 35 per cent).[38] The current personal allowance is only £89 a week. A high tax-free personal allowance would lift millions out of direct tax, prevent a pointless merry-go-round of tax and benefits and would send a simple and popular political message (why *should* those on the minimum wage pay tax?). Nor does it need to be prohibitively expensive. Raising the income tax threshold to £7500, or £15,000 for couples, would cost £10 billion.[39] Not cheap, but affordable over a parliament. Reducing the 10p starting rate of tax to 0p would cost less than £6 billion (only 1 per cent of total managed expenditure with compensatory changes in tax credits possible).[40] Taking pensioners out of tax or out of the starting tax is even more affordable. These must be the stated aims of Fair Conservative tax policy for the next decade.

2   **A Fair Chance in Life.** There are important and necessary
steps ahead to give control of education and school choice
back to parents. As Blair edges his way to this ineluctable
conclusion, we should not kid ourselves that our views on
parental choice will be either immediately popular or
unique. Why not shift our focus from the early steps
towards parental choice (which Labour is likely, painfully,
to take) to how we can help poorer and less well-educated
parents and children prosper within the new choice-based
framework? This will mean that the route to choice we
take will not be based (as it started to be in the 1980s and
1990s) on opt-outs for the fortunate but on choice for all.
It will probably focus more on parental and less on school
choice to avoid leaving the least prosperous to sink on
their own. This might actually mean making *more*
scholarships and competitive grants available only to the
least well off or in certain areas and schools. It might
mean providing weighted additional funding in the
poorest areas, or summer schools targeted on some
schools or poor areas. It will mean putting real energy
into ensuring that selection does not increase inequality,
putting real vigour into explaining the positive role for
government within a decentralised, choice-led, largely
non-state-delivered education system.

3   **A Fair Deal on Crime.** Walk down a shopping street or
round an estate in a less prosperous part of Britain (and I
have many times) and you encounter a degree of
frustration with the criminal justice system unknown in
middle England. There is a level of systemic anger with
the lenient sentences and police indifference which recent
(welcome) reforms have barely moved.[41] One answer,
popular in the party and potentially with voters, is to give
communities more direct control over either criminal
justice or local policing or both – thus seizing decision-
making back from an insipid and timid bureaucracy into

the hands of people who actually suffer from crime. Hard to argue against (why *shouldn't* voters control this?), this may be an idea whose time has come. It has been argued for (in different forms) from both left and right and taps into powerful and profound public emotions.[42] One associated point. Any Conservative home secretary will understand that punishment for crime is about deterrence and, well, punishment as well as rehabilitation. But the re-offending rates of released prisoners and the standards of much prison education are a national disgrace. Picking up on the theme of compulsory drugs rehabilitation in the 2005 manifesto, is there a case for compulsory (and better) prison education? This will cost more. But it may be a case of spend a pound to save ten. This may be the sort of tough proposal that signals that we care too.

4   **Fair Welfare that Works.** The British welfare system is a disgrace. It helps trap the huge majority of recipients, millions of our fellow citizens, out of work and on benefits for years at a time.[43] Attempts to reform have had little success. Most Conservative reforms involved merely paring away at rights and benefit levels leaving the majority of recipients worse off and little better able to find a job.[44] Labour has done no better. They squandered their opportunity in 1997, have extended means testing, left millions marooned on incapacity benefit and have run the New Deal so badly that youth re-employment rates have in fact declined while some schemes (the New Deal for Lone Parents, for instance) actually impair job-finding success. Meanwhile state-incentivised but privately or charitably run active job-find schemes are noticeably more effective at helping job seekers find work both in the UK and abroad. They don't do this by filing away at benefit levels or by being 'tough' (though they can be when necessary). They do it by rapidly providing better advice and assistance to place people into work quickly. It

is a crime that so many people's lives are being wasted. Labour's Welfare to Work has missed the bus. It is time for Fair Welfare that is not hung up on state delivery and that *does* work.

5 **A Fair Britain.** In the US, George Bush's administration has revived and improved the concept of 'enterprise zones' with his Gulf Opportunity Zone tax breaks and regulatory rollbacks to lure entrepreneurs into the hurricane-hit South. During the 1990s, many republican governors also placed great emphasis on urban renewal and positive programmes of low tax, targeted government support and voluntary sector action.[45] Should we be using the same models in the poorer parts of Britain? Conservatives should be outraged by the geographic unfairness of Britain and determined to do something about it. We often talk about the electoral Conservative flight from the cities. Surely credible policies to enrich Britain's regional towns and cities are the best and the most proper response?

Michael Howard used 11 words to define his manifesto. Let me set out an alternative first 11 to define Fair Conservatism (with two players kept on, no counting of the ampersands and one reserve added to the list to make 12!).

Fair Conservatism is . . .

o one nation
o sharing opportunity
o spreading wealth
o fairer schools & hospitals
o fair tax & policing.

These words are, no doubt, not the best available. But they do have two advantages. They are inoffensive to our core voters. And they are addressed to the four million Britons we need to win over if we are going to win an election robustly. Just as Labour appropriated our policies (or claimed to) so we must show that our ends are compatible with those of some (not all) supposedly left-wing voters. For, in opposition, what your policies say about *you* is arguably more important than what you say about your policy.

The phrase 'one nation' is a particularly powerful one. Conservatives neglect it at their peril. Uniquely among descriptions of Conservative philosophy it is both broadly known and widely understood. It is taken as meaning 'being a good bloke, if a Conservative, who means well in politics and wants to help people'. Why on earth do we not deploy it? I have lost track of the number of times, trudging the streets, when I have been told 'You need to be more one-nation conservatives. Then I might vote for you.' Possibly, just possibly, the voters are trying to tell us something. Possibly we should even listen.

Don't get me wrong. Our core focus points of individual freedom, low tax and the reform and outsourcing of public services are good and necessary ones. But they have to be British and to look British. They have to meet British voters' tastes and preferences. And they have to offer a real path to success for *everyone* in society not just the middle classes. At the moment too many of them still don't. Fair Conservatism must. You can't fit an American hot dog into a British sausage sandwich. People won't like it. And the mustard will squirt in your face. We should stop trying.

5. Be consistent

Consider two apparently disconnected problems.

First, modern British political debate is an argument inside a china thimble. Every day, everywhere, we discuss *what* we pay for, *which* public services need to be reformed, *what* the reforms should be.

But will we have the money? If unchecked, at least three profound long-term concerns could shatter our contentment and bring us crashing back into the crisis politics of the 1970s. All are well known. None are sufficiently considered.

- O The first is loosely termed 'globalisation'. It is such a well-rubbed cliché that it obscures the grim reality. Many other countries (China and India are the most discussed) are not just cheaper than us. They are increasingly smarter too. And, thanks to modern technology, they can do a lot more than wire our phones and mould our toys. They can run our banks, conduct sophisticated overnight analysis and even provide a remote variant of middle management. Unless we get very good, work very hard and get much smarter Britain is facing (again) a long future of relative decline. We need *all* of Britain to be part of this struggle. We cannot just rely on the South East and on financial services. Thatcher's revolution needs to be revisited once a generation. But it needs to be extended to the whole country as the challenges of 'globalisation' grow sharper and more severe.

○ Second, every day in every town in Britain a doctor or nurse performs a small miracle and saves the life of someone in their 70s, 80s or 90s – to the immense joy and pleasure of these people and their families. But we can't duck the issue much longer. Paying for pensions and healthcare will mean working longer, saving more and restructuring our economy. Germany and the US are arguably actuarially bust. The only reason we are not is because we conned a generation into thinking they were insured and are now treating them with miserly unconcern. This meanness is now ending. But instead Labour has destroyed the occupational pension. Whatever we do, getting out of this mess *will* cost money. And it *does* need a solution. We need to be prepared to examine the issue at length and to sketch out bold moves on using tax to encourage savings (as David Willetts has already begun to do).

○ Finally, the environment. The issues are too well known to need repeating. The threat is clear. But we are too shy. The environment is not a left-wing issue. Potential and actual Conservatives up and down the country are passionately committed to a range of issues from preserving their local spinney to encouraging recycling. And pricing and market mechanisms (once derided) have established themselves as a core part of the solution. The environment should be one of our big issues. Again, this is the right as well as the smart thing to do (look at the polls about what younger voters care about).

Take a second problem. The main thrust of voters' criticisms of the Conservative Party is no longer that they think we are out of touch. They just think that we are Machiavellian say-anythings: 64 per cent of non-Conservative voters believe we are too opportunistic. The figure is even higher for 'Generation Gap' – 68 per cent. In contrast only (a terrifying but still relatively modest) 39 per cent (and 44 per cent of 'Generation Gap') think that we are bigoted (see figure 6).[46]

So there are big long-term problems facing Britain. And we are seen as too short-termist. Of course the solution is to make the two problems one.

Over the next three years, Fair Conservatism must etch for itself a reputation as the thoughtful party, as the long-term party, as the intellectually bold party. Commentators should concede: 'whatever else you say about them, the Conservatives are trying to grapple with some of the big issues facing Britain and the West'.

Why not establish a series of explicitly long-term policy commissions to examine Conservatism's approach to these challenges and to sketch out solutions? These should be well signalled and very clearly focused on the longer term. They could even be cross-party. Their answers should inform, but not dictate, policy for the next election.

This process should be part of a broader philosophical push over the next three years to define a middle way for the UK between the corporatism of Europe and the less fettered capitalism of the US. The British people may not behave like Americans. But they certainly don't behave like the French or Germans either. We have long ago accepted the sort of painful realities that much of Europe is still grappling with. Let us make a virtue of this and evolve a clearly British middle way which can confront our long-term challenges.[47] Lest this sound unpleasantly reminiscent of the, ultimately unsuccessful, Blairite 'third way' – remember New Labour's project has been crippled by its inability to reform the public sector and its obsession with central government. We do not need to be.

You never know. Raising real issues of real concern to the country might be the most self-interested thing to do. Look at the broad plaudits won by David Willetts's 2005 election proposals to encourage savings via the tax system. Many years ago an important British businessman told me 'being consistently decent is the smartest, most self-interested thing to be'.

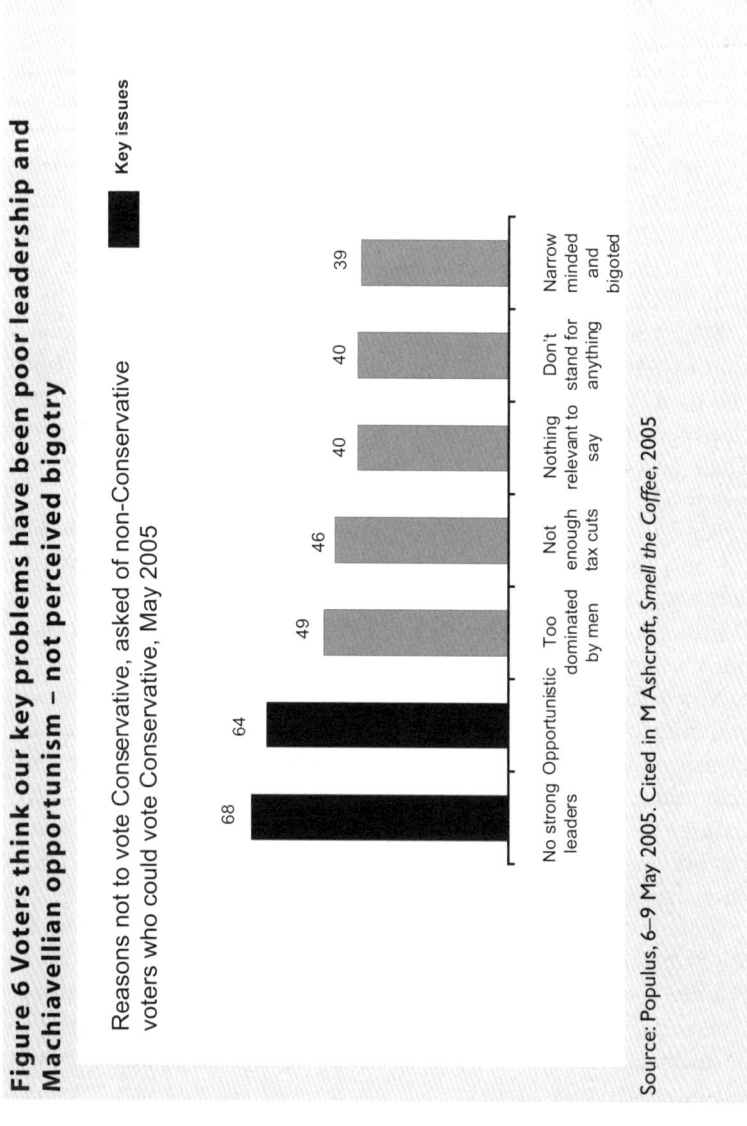

Figure 6 Voters think our key problems have been poor leadership and Machiavellian opportunism – not perceived bigotry

Reasons not to vote Conservative, asked of non-Conservative voters who could vote Conservative, May 2005

Key issues

No strong leaders	Opportunistic	Too dominated by men	Not enough tax cuts	Nothing relevant to say	Don't stand for anything	Narrow minded and bigoted
68	64	49	46	40	40	39

Source: Populus, 6–9 May 2005. Cited in M Ashcroft, *Smell the Coffee*, 2005

6. What winners do

What Blair did

The stock response of many Conservatives when asked if we should study or copy what Tony Blair achieved is a straight 'no'. If you don't believe me, try it.

But why not? In the space of less than three years he polished up a tarnished political brand into a lustrous new one. Our brand is certainly tarnished (remember, in 2005 attribution halves support for some Conservative policies).[48] It certainly needs re-burnishing. The Blair effect seems, to put it mildly, a reasonably relevant case study.

A lot has been written about what Blair did and how he did it. Much of the detail hides the essential point. This is very simple. In his language and in his phrases, in his sound-bites and in his policy, Tony Blair addressed the fears, concerns and aspirations of those who did not vote Labour. Look at a 1995 speech to the CBI:

I reject the rampant laissez-faire of those who believe government has no role in a productive economy; and I reject too, as out of date and impractical, the re-creation or importation of a model of the corporate state popular a generation ago. Today the role of government is not to command but to facilitate, and to do so in partnership with industry in limited but key areas. This is not a matter of ideology but of national interest. The philosophy of one Britain, one nation, in which we put behind us the old debates and focus on what we know needs to be done.[49]

It is easy to cringe (what does all this hot air *mean?*). But what Tony Blair is doing is very important. He is taking a quintessentially 'right-wing' problem (the economy), using 'right-wing' language to describe it ('the role of government is not to command') and using centrist or even right-wing language to map out the solutions ('the philosophy of one Britain, one nation').

However, in one sense Tony Blair is being scrupulously honest here. For, *the solutions remain left wing* (even if far less so than in the 1980s). State 'facilitation' can easily turn into state bullying. As we now know, Labour's economic 'facilitation' involves £125 billion of new tax rises and £40 billion of new regulations. This is hardly right wing. But that is to miss the point. Blair showed that he understood the problems in terms that were anathema to most of his party. He even proposed solutions far more left wing than the alternative available (ie the Conservatives) in terms that were traditionally at least centrist.

There is a lesson here for the Conservative Party. *Because we still don't do this.* After 13 years of growth, the issues at the top of most people's vote-impacting worry list (the NHS, education) are largely 'left wing'. This is particularly true for 'Generation Gap'. The Conservative Party has therefore (correctly) concentrated on the public sector. But we have done so on our terms and in our language. This is a mistake. Like Tony Blair, we need to espouse, and keep on espousing, these left-wing problems *in their terms not in ours.*

Our values are too narrow. We need to evince consistent and genuine 'left-wing' anger at poverty and miserable services. They should not still exist. They do still exist. They should not have got worse since 1997. They have got worse since 1997. If we are to follow the successful example of Tony Blair, this is the core insight. Not getting caught up in discussing the finer details of a market mechanism here or an outsourced arrangement there.

What Bush did

George W Bush first ran for public office in 1978. He ran for Congress from West Texas. It was a disaster. He was pilloried for his patrician roots and his Yale education: 'a Yankee carpetbagger with a fancy East Coast education and no roots in the local community . . . born with a silver boot up his ass'.[50]

George W Bush ran for governor of Texas in 1994. It was a triumph. He won by 53 to 46 per cent – the biggest margin in 20 years. *En route*, he out-Texaned a true Texas-born incumbent (Ann Richards) with an impeccable pedigree (her Texanisms had been collected into a book) and a nice line in put-downs (she had said of Bush's father, 'Poor George, he just can't help it' and dismissed Dubya variously as 'Shrub', 'Junior', 'Prince George' and 'the wind-up-doll').

What had happened? How on earth had the preppy ugly duckling turned into the Texan swan? Part of the answer, of course, was that Bush had hired one of the best guns in the business, Karl Rove.

But Bush had also done something to himself. He had become the anti-politician's politician. He had learnt how to use his language and his persona (even his flaws) to mirror Texas to itself. He visited rural towns in eelskin boots and a Texas Farm Bureau jacket. He hung out with – and was funded by – former Texas Cowboys and their coaches. By, literally, representing Texas to itself, he was able to break down the doors of the governor's mansion.

Bush had also learnt how to keep a political coalition together by giving just enough 'red meat' to his core support and no more. His proposals included requiring teenage girls who wanted an abortion to get their parents' permission. But that was all.

Bush even learnt to express his radical political aspirations in congenial terms. 'Government does not have a monopoly on compassion' was his catchphrase of the campaign – as it was to be when he ran for the White House. Reforming education was termed as 'no child left behind', not introducing vouchers and choice.[51] Above all, Bush learnt how to reach beyond target voters – to non-white voters for instance – not because he expected many of them to vote for him (few do) but because by doing so he reassures middle America.

Is there an implication for the Conservative Party? You bet. We need to be the anti-politician's politicians too:

○ Don't let your message to core voters alienate everyone else.

○ Don't be too smart – talk to all the nation (including the poor) not just to a cleverly defined core and target vote. If you don't care about most people, the voters will sniff you out.

○ Don't talk weirdly. Use the language of everyday life – not the strident, acerbic tones of the professional politician.

The Liberal Democrats are the masters of being the anti-political politicians in British politics. That's why most voters think Charles Kennedy is a good bloke. That's why 66 per cent think the Liberal Democrats are honest and principled, 52 per cent that they share their values – including 55 per cent of 'Generation Gap'.[52]

Until the registers of criticism, mock-shock and sarcasm are replaced with humour, gentleness and sweet reason, there will be few 'good blokes' in the public eye view of the Conservative Party.

Centre. Centre. Centre.

The data is obsessively, almost manically, clear. No political party can win on its own. No party since the war has won without attracting floating voters who have, did or would consider voting for another party. Now more than ever. We have to talk to the middle. We have to share the values of the centre ground. Only one voter in three thinks we currently do.[53]

David Frum, a former speechwriter to President Bush, reportedly once said: 'When a political party offers the voters ham and eggs and the voters say, "No thanks", its first instinct is to say, "OK then – how about double ham and double eggs?"'.[54] He is right. And it is time to change the menu. We need to relearn how to pick 'red meat' topics (crime and fair tax for instance), which attract without repelling. By contrast we must cease to highlight topics (above all immigration) which do not affect votes cast but which underline negative perceptions about us.

Just to be very clear, only 12 per cent of voters in key seats say immigration is *the* key issue on which they vote – including only 5 per cent of Labour, Liberal Democrat and floating voters. Only 9 per cent of 'Generation Gap' voters under 34 think it is *the* critical issue. That is not much of a potential dividend when you realise that a tough stance on immigration either repels floating voters when they do not prioritise the issue (and in most surveys around 60 per cent of floating voters don't) or embarrasses them even when they do. Just to show how little traction the issue has: those who thought the Tories best on immigration and asylum (most people did) *and* that Labour were best on the economy (again, most people did) voted 48 per cent Labour and 19 per cent Tory.[55] Ask the question a different way and liberal attitudes on race relations *do* still prevail: 69 per cent think it is a good thing that Britain is 'multi-racial'. Hardly surprisingly that since 2001 on average over 40 per cent of AB voters have thought Conservatives 'too right wing'.[56] Immigration is a core vote strategy with a toxic sting.[57]

Unless we are talking to the centre of British politics we are talking to the mirror. Again.

7. A mile wide not a mile deep

The Conservative Party is meant to be the party with a sense of history. Some should go back to their text books. The most culturally astute and politically successful Conservative leaders have always taken a broad view of their party's aims, tenets, methods and beliefs. Orderly change. The imperfection of people, society and government. The limit to the power of reason and government. Prosperity and property. Nation. Liberty and law. A strong but limited state.[58]

Look at some Conservatives who could win elections.

Take Benjamin Disraeli. He made his life's work defining the Conservative Party against the Liberals as the Party of the Nation. Nation meant Empire. But it also meant plain English common sense against the cold economics of the Liberals (whom Disraeli dismissed as the 'philosophic party').[59] Above all, nation also meant duty and service to the poorest. Disraeli's novel *Sybil* excoriates the Liberals for creating a Britain of 'two nations'. It stands alongside Dickens and Gaskell as one of the great pieces of nineteenth-century social literature. Remember Charles Booth's interest in the poor made him a Conservative.

Take Stanley Baldwin – playing on the themes of security and calm gentility in his tweed suit and country walks. Condemned now for being an appeaser (Churchill said it would have been better for Britain had he never lived), at the time he seemed rather a world statesman steering a fractious continent to peace. His face featured on the cover of *Time* magazine and his elegy to the English countryside has entered the political lexicon:

> *The sounds of England, the tinkle of the hammer on the anvil in the country smithy, the corncrake on a dewy morning, the sound of a scythe against a whetstone and the sight of a ploughteam coming across the brow of a hill . . . for centuries the one eternal sight of England.*[60]

Take Harold Macmillan. Unfashionable now in the Conservative Party for his conciliation with socialism, at another level his political achievement was breathtaking. He used rising incomes and his own calm and political sang-froid to overcome Suez, resignations, an ignominious end of Empire and a perilous relative collapse of Britain's power and wealth against enemies old (France and Germany) and new (Russia). John Major was to perish trying to accommodate Britain and the Conservative Party to far more pusillanimous perils. Macmillan had many tricks up his Edwardian sleeves. He did not preach (he once said that if people want morality, they should seek it from their archbishop). And he *did* evince a widely credited concern for the less well off:

> *When I am told . . . that inflation can be cured or arrested only by returning to substantial or even massive unemployment, I reject that utterly.*[61]

Above all, take Margaret Thatcher:

> *For me, the heart of politics is not political theory, it is people and how they want to live their lives. No one who has lived in this country during the last five years can fail to be aware of how the balance of our society has been increasingly tilted in favour of the State at the expense of individual freedom. . . . The things that we have in common as a nation far outnumber those that set us apart.*[62]

Nation. Duty. Service. Order. Common sense. Tradition. An aesthetic sense of Britain. Reassurance. Calm. Charity. Real people. The themes of successful Conservatism are rich and varied. Fair Conservatism must rediscover them all. We are not *just* about freedom and enterprise and economic revolution.

The citation from Mrs Thatcher is particularly instructive. It is from her 1979 manifesto. This was the manifesto that was to usher in the most radical 11 years of British government since the war and the most successful peace-time government for well over a century.

Is it a revolutionary text? No. It is couched in terms of 'people' and 'lives'. Even anodyne abstractions such as 'freedom' are used sparingly. Reasonability prevails.

The free market is a tool in achieving our ends. Indeed, it is the critical tool. But it is not the end in itself. To define a free market as the end is to speak in terms of an abstraction alien to the lives of most Britons, most of the time. Most British voters do not know what *laissez-faire* means. They certainly do not feel like giving their vote to it. To talk too much of economics is to sound extreme or obsessive – a sort of demented modern Mr Gradgrind trapped in the prism of his own logic.

Most Conservative Party leaders understand this. Much of the 2005 Conservative manifesto was actually a masterpiece of moderation, reason and sobriety. But does everyone undestand it? There are too many examples of Conservative representatives talking to the media in terms that return too readily to a stock and unhelpful vocabulary of freedom, markets, individuality or destruction in the public services.

This is not enough. The conception of the party it betrays, the conception of our aims and our mission is too narrow. We are not *just* old-style Manchester Liberals.

We need to broaden our vision and lengthen our hopes for our fellow citizens. Money may be how we 'keep count' in life. But it is not how most of us judge happiness or goodness. At least not in Britain. Quality of life and compassion matters too. Our language needs to show that we understand that – just as the language of successful Conservatives has always done.

Winston Churchill wrote that 'in my many elections I have learnt to know and honour the people of this island. They are good through and through.'[63]

We have sometimes forgotten that. Fair Conservatism must remember.

8. Six reasons to hope

British Conservatism has always contained within it an element that is depressed, nostalgic for the past, melancholy for the future. It has certainly been easy to give in to moods of Oakeshottian depression during 2005. And there have certainly been soothsayers intoning us to do so.

We must not listen. We can be proud, positive and hopeful.

We certainly have a lot of work, a lot of change to define. And it will be hard to do it. But there are six big reasons to hope.

First of all, never forget England is ours.

We won more votes in England (8.12 million) than Labour (8.04 million) or the Liberal Democrats (5.2 million). A pitiful 18,000 votes in the right places would have brought us a crucial 30 additional seats. Barely more votes (39,000) would have brought us 20 more – enough to be within striking distance of a hung parliament. Achieving a hung parliament, in short, could be moderately easy.[64]

Second, winning is possible. The votes *are* still there to be won.

Stubbornly almost, despite all our failures, there are still a staggering 9.1 million British adults who did not vote or did not vote Conservative in 2005 and who *would* be prepared to do so. Of these (and based on another poll) anything up to 1.8 million consider themselves 'likely' Conservative voters – enough to win an election with a 1992-scale majority. Better still, a disproportionately high number of these potential voters are young or 'Generation Gap' voters. Winning these votes is hard work. But the voters are shouting at us: 'it can be done'.[65]

Third, Conservatives should be very nervous of but should not be paralysed by the Liberal threat.

It cuts both ways. It *is* true that Liberal votes are responsible for 18 of our 31 parliamentary gains.[66] But this way of winning seats is hardly novel to the Conservative Party. In 1983, the combined Alliance and Labour vote was greater than the Conservative vote in scores of Conservative-held seats. The Liberal Democrats are now more immediately threatening in Labour seats (five 'micro-marginals' with majorities of less than 2000) than they are in Conservative ones (only three 'micro-marginals'). In a further 16 seats a Liberal gain of less than 1000 votes would deliver the seat to Conservative candidates. As Labour puts it, a vote for Kennedy really could put us in. Margaret Thatcher used the same trick.

Fourth, we have ever more troops on the ground.

Since 2002 alone, let alone the dark nadir of the late 1990s, the number of Conservative councillors has increased by 15 per cent from 7109 to 8064 (see figure 7). This matters. Not just because of local government control. But because, as any activist of any party will tell you, councillors (particularly young ones and particularly ones who think they have to *fight* for their seats) are the guts and sinew in a local party's vote-grabbing tendencies. They live round the corner. They know the streets. They need the canvass records up to date from election to election. Young councillors who could lose are what you need. And the Conservatives have got them in spades. Our army is not just bigger than it used to be. It's younger and better motivated.

Fifth, we increasingly even know what we are doing.

In 1997 I spent election day in Bedford, then a Conservative-held marginal with a notional majority of 2500 votes.[67] It was like being trapped behind enemy lines. There was no central control. No one knew where to send me. No one knew where or when telling results would come through (many never would; there was no one there). I was ultimately sent to one ward being run by one elderly former

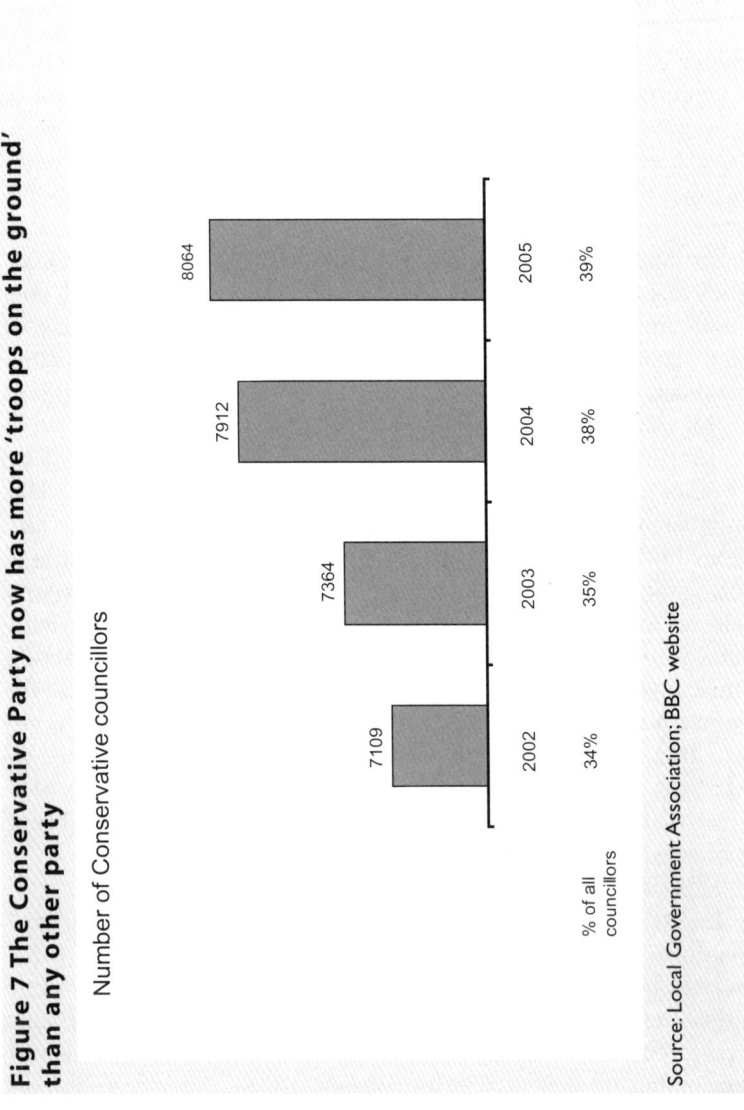

Figure 7 The Conservative Party now has more 'troops on the ground' than any other party

Number of Conservative councillors

	2002	2003	2004	2005
	7109	7364	7912	8064
% of all councillors	34%	35%	38%	39%

Source: Local Government Association; BBC website

councillor and his even more elderly mother. There were Conservative posters in the window. There was no other sign of political activity. Eventually, after a cup of tea, I was sent alone to knock up a thin list of canvass returns. Most had not been canvassed for several years. As I wandered pathetically around from street to street, a team of a dozen red-rosetted, red-rosed Labour activists swept past me knocking, it seemed, on every other door in the street. Within minutes they were finished and on to the next street. I felt like a *maquisard* flinging pebbles ineffectually at a tank.

In 2005, I spent election day in Hammersmith and Fulham – a Labour-held marginal of just over 2000. The contrast was thunderous. A rigorous and consistent campaign. Effective personalisation of politics – with letters from the candidate targeted at (for instance) car owners (due to the congestion charge), inhabitants of certain streets (with specific local crime problems) or council leaseholders (due to high service charges). A well-known local candidate, Greg Hands, with a proven council track record. True doorstep politics. Personal follow-up by the candidate to *all* canvassed voters. Better leaflets. Complete knowledge of voters and potential voters. True understanding of local themes and issues – built up over years of hard graft. Rapid deployment of volunteers as needed around the constituency. The Labour candidate, spotted dallying outside a local supermarket, looked less like a future MP and more like a bemused spectator as dozens of blue rosettes swarmed past at speed.[68]

The contrast is personal. But it illustrates a wider trend. Like running a supermarket, much political success is in the detail. Local effort works.[69] In some regions (above all, London) the interaction of better local officials, wiser central support together with a rejuvenated and more technically savvy local hierarchy has wrestled the campaigning advantage back from Labour and the Liberal Democrats.

But not in all regions. 2005 general election horror stories abound from target seats – particularly in the north. Of bussed-in activists hanging around for hours. Of volunteers given incorrect canvassing cards and no briefing. Of poorly managed local records. The discrepancy is (arguably) visible in the local results where much of the north continued to lose Conservative voters despite already being at what seemed like rock bottom. 'Best practice' needs dispersing from its southern and metropolitan heartland. This can and should be the focus of organisational renewal for the Conservative Party itself. Given the way that the electoral landscape – social, geographical and local – is changing, working hard at such renewal could bring hard returns relatively quickly.

Finally, many Conservatives are thinking hard, creatively and intelligently about what we should do to win the next election – and doing something about it. A British general in 1940 once complained that he had been sent to fight the last war not this one. I think we are *not* about to make that mistake. Ideas abound within the parliamentary and voluntary wings of the party. The recent leadership campaign has been by far the most invigorating and enriching of the four since 1997. Party supporters and think tanks, voluntary organisations and party officials are commissioning polls, studying politics abroad and analysing the recent election with a new degree of rigour and science.

There are real ideas for change, too. Here are a few of the more notable:

○   A new logo. The current torch looks like a cross between a Stalinist poster and a gym advertisement. We would be better off with something that had cultural or environmental overtones: a stylised map of Britain perhaps or an oak tree.

○   A new name. Fair Conservatives. Modern Conservatives. Compassionate Conservatives.

○   Start to train activists properly rather as the Republican political action committee (GOPAC) did in the US – at least one non-party organisation, the Young Britons Foundation, has already been set up to achieve this.

No one should be complacent. But no one should despair, either. With a new language and a revised purpose we have many of the tools to finish the job. While many politicians, journalists and commentators have become used to the idea that the Conservative Party teeters on the edge of oblivion, internally it is closer to rediscovering its effectiveness than many realise.

9. Conclusion: Fair Conservatism

Take two modern visions of Britain.

If you walk up the hill from Pier Head on the River Mersey you pass the Victorian streets and offices of central Liverpool until you reach the open space of William Brown Street. Here the Walker Art Gallery and the Liverpool Museum and Library stare down the hill towards Birkenhead. Above them, the magnificent St George's Hall dominates the town in all directions. On the east side, like Ozymandias, stands a statue of Disraeli enrobed in courtly ermine, a monument to Victorian pride and civic confidence. But the boundless and bare expanse around Disraeli's bronze feet is (still) a sand of semi-vandalised public parks, boarded-up offices, half-full hotels and empty streets.

There is another Britain.

Walk down Bond Street or High Street Kensington in London, or the high street of any one of ten dozen towns in southern England, and you can barely move without tumbling over the trappings of banking and commercial success: restaurants and bars without cease; kitchen design shops; chromed shop fronts; three-wheeled prams costing nearly 10 per cent of a single pensioner's entire annual income.

Stop to think about it (most of us don't) and the inequality is staggering. The unfairness is deeper still. Beneath the surface and the chrome are vastly different chances of getting on and up. The babies in the three-wheeled prams (assuming they are one of the nearly 10 per cent who are educated privately) will have more money lavished on them in one year than most babies born in central Liverpool have in ten.

And the government? It watches helpless – still mesmerised by some of its own supporters and unable to execute real reform. For all its tough talk on liberating the private sector, it has created only 17 city academies. It is hardly the 'third way' revolution we were promised. Fair Conservatism is being angry about this unholy contrast. Fair Conservatism is being politely furious at the government's failure to resolve it. Fair Conservatism is pledging ourselves to the task of doing something about it – not by pulling down the wealthy but by helping up the weak. Fair Conservatism is ending the outrageous anomaly that the poor pay a *higher* proportion of their income in taxes than the middle classes. Fair Conservatism is about extending the 1980s' revolution to the whole country so that we can all meet the challenges of globalisation, an ageing population and environmental change. Together. Fair Conservatism is about lowering the barriers to achievement – above all where those barriers are highest. Fair Conservatism is about liberating government time and energy. Twenty men and women in Whitehall cannot micro-manage a third of the economy. They should not try. The idea has only to be stated to be seen to be absurd. But in changing government we have to be utterly focused on social justice so that the least well off are never the victims of change.

Ultimately, though, Fair Conservatism must be a sense of duty and civic and communal pride. Meeting, over the years, hundreds of Conservative activists, young and old, rich and poor, I have been struck consistently by the range and breadth of the charities and local organisations they run and staff. We need to propel this private local sense of communal duty into the public perception of our party.

It was, after all, this spirit that inspired Charles Booth. This was why he devoted a decade to studying the lives of the urban poor, 100 years ago. This was the spirit which made him a Conservative.

Until Charles Booth's motivation, choice, priorities and actions are surprising neither to ourselves, nor to others, then Conservatives have little chance of receiving again the keys of government.

Notes

1   See: www.cameroncampaign.org (accessed 9 Nov 2005).
2   British competitiveness has fallen in both the World Economic Forum and the Heritage Foundation rankings since 1997. See note 6 re decline in equality.
3   M Booth, *Charles Booth – A Memoir* (London: Macmillan, 1918); R O'Day and D Englander, *Mr. Charles Booth's Inquiry: Life and labour of the people in London reconsidered* (London: Hambledon & London Ltd, 1992).
4   W Booth, *In Darkest England and the Way Out* (London: Funk and Wagnalls, 1890).
5   Information on Merthyr Tydfil from *Local Labour Force Survey*, 2004, and Welsh Assembly survey into incapacity benefit, 2001.
6   *Regional Trends*, 1995, 2004. *Family Resources Survey*, 2004. Institute for Fiscal Studies, *Election Briefing: Living standards, inequality and poverty* (London: IFS, 2005).
7   Department of Work and Pensions. Statistics and Research Resource Centre.
8   M Novak, *The New Consensus on Family Welfare* (Washington, DC: American Enterprise Institute, 1987).
9   C Lakin, *The Effects of Taxes & Benefits on Household Income, 2001–2002* (London: Office for National Statistics, 2003); cited in R Lea, *The Price of the Profligate Chancellor: Higher taxes to come* (London: Centre for Policy Studies, 2004). N Blackwell, *Take Poor Families Out of Tax* (London: CPS, 2005).
10 Greater London Authority, *London Divided* (London: GLA, 2002).
11 'Students count multiple A grades', BBC News, 18 Aug 2005.
12 *British Social Attitudes*; see: www.britsocat.com (accessed 9 Nov 2005).
13 Ibid.
14 M Ashcroft, *Smell the Coffee – A Wake Up Call for the Conservative Party* (2005); available at: www.politicos.co.uk/item.jsp?ID=5322 (accessed 10 Nov 2005).
15 Pew Global Attitudes Project, *Views of a Changing World* (Washington, DC: PewResearchCentre, 2003).

16   Institute for Fiscal Studies, *Election Briefing;* and *Households Below Average Income 2003/04*, Table 7.1.
17   BBC website. Conservative Conference 2003 section.
18   See E Roche, 'Words for the wise', *Harvard Business Review* (Jan 2001).
19   T Blair, speech accepting leadership of the Labour Party (21 July 1994), in *New Britain: My vision of a young country* (London: Fourth Estate, 1996).
20   Populus (May 2005), YouGov (April 2005) and Bow Group Private Polling (2005).
21   Populus (May 2005).
22   MORI Final Aggregate Analysis; see: www.mori.com (accessed 9 Nov 2005).
23   Ibid.
24   Office for National Statistics, *Social Trends, 2005* (London: ONS, 2005).
25   4% would bring 'Generation Gap' voting into line with that of others below 45; 200,000 assumes a 60% turnout; assumes uniform swing. Figures derived from BBC Election 2005 website.
26   *British Social Attitudes;* see: www.britsocat.com (accessed 9 Nov 2005); private polling.
27   *British Social Attitudes.*
28   Ibid.
29   George Orwell, *The Lion and the Unicorn* (London: Penguin Books, 1982; first publ. 1941).
30   *British Social Attitudes;* private polling.
31   Populus (Jan 2005, May 2005).
32   *British Social Attitudes.*
33   Pew Global Attitudes Project, *Views of a Changing World.*
34   *Direct Democracy: An agenda for a new model party* (London: Direct Democracy, 2005).
35   Office of the Deputy Prime Minister, *Turnout at Local Election* (London: ODPM, May 2002).
36   School Choice For All conference, 27 Apr 2004; see: www.reform.co.uk (accessed 9 Nov 2005).
37   *British Social Attitudes.*
38   Lakin, *The Effects of Taxes & Benefits on Household Income, 2001–2002.*
39   Blackwell, *Take Poor Families Out of Tax.*
40   Figures calculated using HM Treasury's Ready Tax Reckoner.
41   This impression is backed up by sound polling data. The public wants tougher sentences and believes the police are the least effective of the three emergency services. W Hatter, *Public Attitudes to Policing* (London: MORI, 2000); see: www.mori.com and www.britsocat.com (both accessed 9 Nov 2005).
42   For a Conservative variant of some of these ideas, some local control of policing is buried in the Conservative 2005 manifesto. For a left-wing version, see B Rogers, *New Directions in Community Justice* (London: ippr, 2005).
43   For more detail on this point and the proposals in this paragraph see the forthcoming study of welfare by Reform.
44   Peter Lilley's more broadly conceived reforms were an exception to this trend.

45 This is part of the often mentioned 'Compassionate Conservatism' programme pioneered by Marvin Olasky. See 'The US Republicans: lessons for the Conservatives?' in M Garnett and P Lynch (eds), *The Conservatives in Crisis* (Manchester: Manchester University Press, 2003).

46 Populus poll (6–9 May), cited in Ashcroft, *Smell the Coffee*.

47 I owe the phrase 'middle way' in this context to Rupert Darwell.

48 Support for immigration policy falls from 64% to 30% when attributed. Populus (May 2005).

49 T Blair, speech to the annual conference of the Confederation of British Industry (13 Nov 1995), in *New Britain*.

50 J Micklethwait and A Wooldridge, *The Right Nation* (New York: Penguin, 2004).

51 Ibid.

52 Populus (May 2005).

53 Ibid. 34% of voters think Conservatives 'share their values'.

54 V Bogdanor, 'The Tories need a genuine liberal', *Spectator*, 15 Oct 2005.

55 Populus poll of 130 key marginals (10–14 May 2005) cited in Ashcroft, *Smell the Coffee*; Populus (May 2005).

56 See A Tyrie, *Back from the Brink* (London: Parliamentary Mainstream, 2001).

57 The campaign 'Keep the Pound' was just as disastrous in the 2001 campaign. In a post-election Gallup survey, 65% felt Conservatives focused too much on Europe. *Daily Telegraph*, 11 Jun 2001.

58 This list is taken from A Seldon and P Snowden, *A New Conservative Century?* (London: Centre for Policy Studies, 2001).

59 Cited in D Gelernter, 'The inventor of modern conservatism', *Weekly Standard*, 7 Feb 2005.

60 Cited in MJ Wiener, *English Culture and Decline of the Industrial Spirit, 1850–1980* (London: Penguin, 1992).

61 Cited in V Bogdanor, 'Unflappable master of the middle way' (obituary, Harold Macmillan), *Guardian*, 30 Dec 1986.

62 Conservative manifesto, 1979.

63 W Churchill, *Thoughts and Adventures* (London: Thornton Butterworth Limited, 1932).

64 BBC Election 2005 website.

65 Ashcroft, *Smell the Coffee*.

66 BBC Election 2005 website.

67 A notional majority due to boundary changes before the 1997 election.

68 Personal knowledge buttressed by an interview with Greg Smith, the campaign manager.

69 Liberal Democrat MPs who have historically (though no longer) worked harder locally used to have measurably higher job satisfaction rates from voters than Conservative and Labour MPs. See: Tyrie, *Back from the Brink*.

DEMOS – Licence to Publish

THE WORK (AS DEFINED BELOW) IS PROVIDED UNDER THE TERMS OF THIS LICENCE ("LICENCE"). THE WORK IS PROTECTED BY COPYRIGHT AND/OR OTHER APPLICABLE LAW. ANY USE OF THE WORK OTHER THAN AS AUTHORIZED UNDER THIS LICENCE IS PROHIBITED. BY EXERCISING ANY RIGHTS TO THE WORK PROVIDED HERE, YOU ACCEPT AND AGREE TO BE BOUND BY THE TERMS OF THIS LICENCE. DEMOS GRANTS YOU THE RIGHTS CONTAINED HERE IN CONSIDERATION OF YOUR ACCEPTANCE OF SUCH TERMS AND CONDITIONS.

1. **Definitions**
   a **"Collective Work"** means a work, such as a periodical issue, anthology or encyclopedia, in which the Work in its entirety in unmodified form, along with a number of other contributions, constituting separate and independent works in themselves, are assembled into a collective whole. A work that constitutes a Collective Work will not be considered a Derivative Work (as defined below) for the purposes of this Licence.
   b **"Derivative Work"** means a work based upon the Work or upon the Work and other pre-existing works, such as a musical arrangement, dramatization, fictionalization, motion picture version, sound recording, art reproduction, abridgment, condensation, or any other form in which the Work may be recast, transformed, or adapted, except that a work that constitutes a Collective Work or a translation from English into another language will not be considered a Derivative Work for the purpose of this Licence.
   c **"Licensor"** means the individual or entity that offers the Work under the terms of this Licence.
   d **"Original Author"** means the individual or entity who created the Work.
   e **"Work"** means the copyrightable work of authorship offered under the terms of this Licence.
   f **"You"** means an individual or entity exercising rights under this Licence who has not previously violated the terms of this Licence with respect to the Work, or who has received express permission from DEMOS to exercise rights under this Licence despite a previous violation.
2. **Fair Use Rights.** Nothing in this licence is intended to reduce, limit, or restrict any rights arising from fair use, first sale or other limitations on the exclusive rights of the copyright owner under copyright law or other applicable laws.
3. **Licence Grant.** Subject to the terms and conditions of this Licence, Licensor hereby grants You a worldwide, royalty-free, non-exclusive, perpetual (for the duration of the applicable copyright) licence to exercise the rights in the Work as stated below:
   a to reproduce the Work, to incorporate the Work into one or more Collective Works, and to reproduce the Work as incorporated in the Collective Works;
   b to distribute copies or phonorecords of, display publicly, perform publicly, and perform publicly by means of a digital audio transmission the Work including as incorporated in Collective Works;
   The above rights may be exercised in all media and formats whether now known or hereafter devised. The above rights include the right to make such modifications as are technically necessary to exercise the rights in other media and formats. All rights not expressly granted by Licensor are hereby reserved.
4. **Restrictions.** The licence granted in Section 3 above is expressly made subject to and limited by the following restrictions:
   a You may distribute, publicly display, publicly perform, or publicly digitally perform the Work only under the terms of this Licence, and You must include a copy of, or the Uniform Resource Identifier for, this Licence with every copy or phonorecord of the Work You distribute, publicly display, publicly perform, or publicly digitally perform. You may not offer or impose any terms on the Work that alter or restrict the terms of this Licence or the recipients' exercise of the rights granted hereunder. You may not sublicence the Work. You must keep intact all notices that refer to this Licence and to the disclaimer of warranties. You may not distribute, publicly display, publicly perform, or publicly digitally perform the Work with any technological measures that control access or use of the Work in a manner inconsistent with the terms of this Licence Agreement. The above applies to the Work as incorporated in a Collective Work, but this does not require the Collective Work apart from the Work itself to be made subject to the terms of this Licence. If You create a Collective Work, upon notice from any Licencor You must, to the extent practicable, remove from the Collective Work any reference to such Licensor or the Original Author, as requested.
   b You may not exercise any of the rights granted to You in Section 3 above in any manner that is primarily intended for or directed toward commercial advantage or private monetary

compensation. The exchange of the Work for other copyrighted works by means of digital file-sharing or otherwise shall not be considered to be intended for or directed toward commercial advantage or private monetary compensation, provided there is no payment of any monetary compensation in connection with the exchange of copyrighted works.

c If you distribute, publicly display, publicly perform, or publicly digitally perform the Work or any Collective Works, You must keep intact all copyright notices for the Work and give the Original Author credit reasonable to the medium or means You are utilizing by conveying the name (or pseudonym if applicable) of the Original Author if supplied; the title of the Work if supplied. Such credit may be implemented in any reasonable manner; provided, however, that in the case of a Collective Work, at a minimum such credit will appear where any other comparable authorship credit appears and in a manner at least as prominent as such other comparable authorship credit.

5. Representations, Warranties and Disclaimer

a By offering the Work for public release under this Licence, Licensor represents and warrants that, to the best of Licensor's knowledge after reasonable inquiry:

i Licensor has secured all rights in the Work necessary to grant the licence rights hereunder and to permit the lawful exercise of the rights granted hereunder without You having any obligation to pay any royalties, compulsory licence fees, residuals or any other payments;

ii The Work does not infringe the copyright, trademark, publicity rights, common law rights or any other right of any third party or constitute defamation, invasion of privacy or other tortious injury to any third party.

b EXCEPT AS EXPRESSLY STATED IN THIS LICENCE OR OTHERWISE AGREED IN WRITING OR REQUIRED BY APPLICABLE LAW, THE WORK IS LICENCED ON AN "AS IS" BASIS, WITHOUT WARRANTIES OF ANY KIND, EITHER EXPRESS OR IMPLIED INCLUDING, WITHOUT LIMITATION, ANY WARRANTIES REGARDING THE CONTENTS OR ACCURACY OF THE WORK.

6. Limitation on Liability. EXCEPT TO THE EXTENT REQUIRED BY APPLICABLE LAW, AND EXCEPT FOR DAMAGES ARISING FROM LIABILITY TO A THIRD PARTY RESULTING FROM BREACH OF THE WARRANTIES IN SECTION 5, IN NO EVENT WILL LICENSOR BE LIABLE TO YOU ON ANY LEGAL THEORY FOR ANY SPECIAL, INCIDENTAL, CONSEQUENTIAL, PUNITIVE OR EXEMPLARY DAMAGES ARISING OUT OF THIS LICENCE OR THE USE OF THE WORK, EVEN IF LICENSOR HAS BEEN ADVISED OF THE POSSIBILITY OF SUCH DAMAGES.

7. Termination

a This Licence and the rights granted hereunder will terminate automatically upon any breach by You of the terms of this Licence. Individuals or entities who have received Collective Works from You under this Licence, however, will not have their licences terminated provided such individuals or entities remain in full compliance with those licences. Sections 1, 2, 5, 6, 7, and 8 will survive any termination of this Licence.

b Subject to the above terms and conditions, the licence granted here is perpetual (for the duration of the applicable copyright in the Work). Notwithstanding the above, Licensor reserves the right to release the Work under different licence terms or to stop distributing the Work at any time; provided, however that any such election will not serve to withdraw this Licence (or any other licence that has been, or is required to be, granted under the terms of this Licence), and this Licence will continue in full force and effect unless terminated as stated above.

8. Miscellaneous

a Each time You distribute or publicly digitally perform the Work or a Collective Work, DEMOS offers to the recipient a licence to the Work on the same terms and conditions as the licence granted to You under this Licence.

b If any provision of this Licence is invalid or unenforceable under applicable law, it shall not affect the validity or enforceability of the remainder of the terms of this Licence, and without further action by the parties to this agreement, such provision shall be reformed to the minimum extent necessary to make such provision valid and enforceable.

c No term or provision of this Licence shall be deemed waived and no breach consented to unless such waiver or consent shall be in writing and signed by the party to be charged with such waiver or consent.

d This Licence constitutes the entire agreement between the parties with respect to the Work licensed here. There are no understandings, agreements or representations with respect to the Work not specified here. Licensor shall not be bound by any additional provisions that may appear in any communication from You. This Licence may not be modified without the mutual written agreement of DEMOS and You.